It actually is Rocket Science!

Ad astra!

Andreas Raelert

ROCKET SCIENCE

ANDREW RADER

ILLUSTRATION BY GALEN FRAZER

ISBN: 978-0-578-19836-1

EPIC SPACE ADVENTURE AND OTHER SCIENCE BOOKS & GAMES AT
WWW.ANDREW-RADER.COM

10

12b

FIG. 3

$$v(t) = v_0 + v_e \ln \frac{M_0}{M(t)}$$

Earth is a small stage in a vast cosmic arena.

-Carl Sagan

The Universe is vast. We live among billions upon billions of galaxies, each containing billions upon billions of stars. There are more stars in the Universe than all the grains of sand on all the beaches of Earth, and thousands more are born every second.

We are made of stars.
The heavier elements in
our bodies, and everything
around us, were forged
in long extinct stars. The lighter
elements were created at the beginning
of the Universe, 13.8 billion years ago.

You are here

Solar System

Our star, called the Sun, is an ordinary medium-sized star in one corner of a medium-sized galaxy called the Milky Way. Most stars are surrounded by planets, and ours is no exception. Planets form when enough material concentrates together for gravity to compress it into a ball, just like stars.

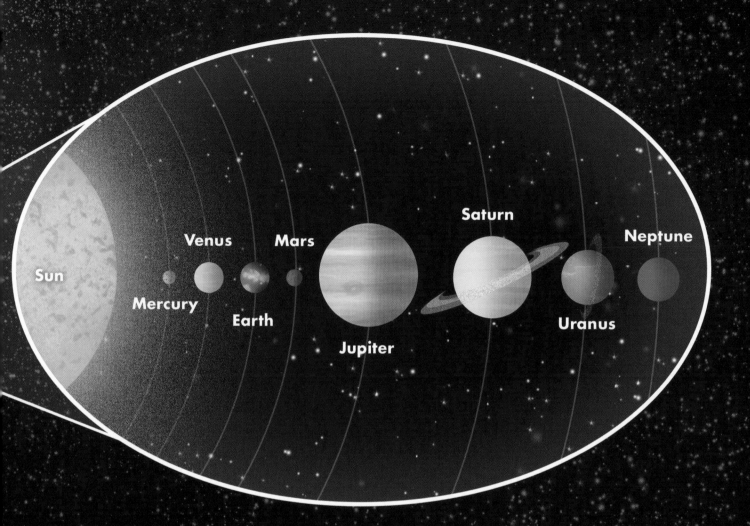

Our solar system contains eight planets, five dwarf planets, hundreds of moons, and millions of smaller bodies ranging from giant asteroids down to tiny specks of dust. Most of the planets are surrounded by moons, with Jupiter and Saturn each having more than sixty!

Earth and Moon

Earth is a medium-sized rocky planet, third from the Sun. What makes Earth special is that it's close enough to the Sun to stay warm, but far enough that it's not too hot. The "Goldilocks" of planets, it's just the right temperature to have oceans of liquid water.

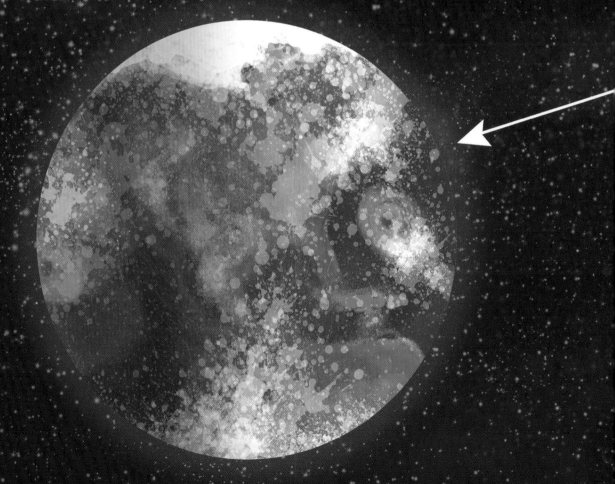

384,400 km
(Earth and Moon not to scale)

Earth's Moon, called Luna, is only the fifth biggest moon, but it is the largest relative to the size of its planet. It's so big that it causes regular tides in Earth's oceans, and lights up the night sky on a full Moon. The Moon probably formed from material ejected when a giant object collided with Earth long ago.

How Rockets Work: Engines

There is no air in space, so we can't use propellers that push against air or balloons that float. Rockets burn mixtures of air and fuel, and push against their own exhaust to accelerate forward. Since there is no air in space to burn, rockets bring their own oxygen.

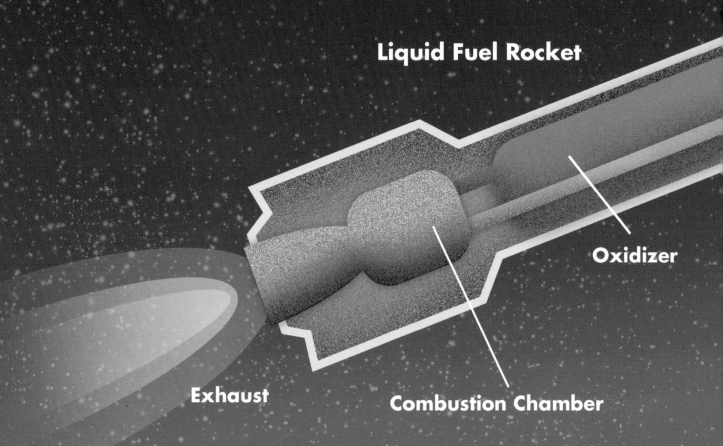

Liquid Fuel Rocket

Oxidizer

Exhaust

Combustion Chamber

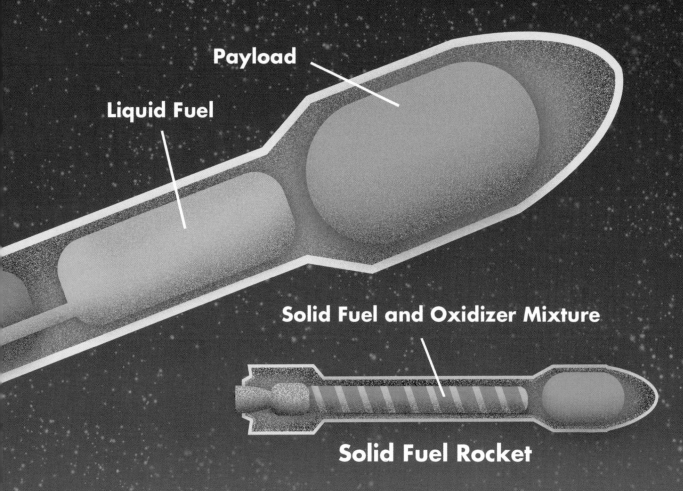

Payload

Liquid Fuel

Solid Fuel and Oxidizer Mixture

Solid Fuel Rocket

Some rockets use oxygen chilled to extremely cold temperatures and stored as liquid. Other rockets use a solid fuel and oxidizer mixture. Both types create a controlled explosion that pushes out exhaust many times faster than a speeding bullet.

Payload

Fairing

Upper Stage

First Stage Center Core (returns to Earth)

First Stage Boosters (return to Earth after using up fuel)

How Rockets Work: Staging

Getting to space is hard, so a rocket must be as light as possible. One way to make a rocket lighter is to divide the rocket into segments, and jettison the segments that have already burned their fuel and oxidizer.

For a rocket, these segments are called "stages". Each stage has its own fuel tank, oxidizer supply, and engine(s). All of the lower stages are shed during flight, so that only the smallest and lightest stage reaches orbit.

How Rockets Work: Landing

Since the beginning of spaceflight, most rockets have thrown away their stages to break up in the atmosphere. This was done for simplicity and to maximize performance, but it is very expensive because it means that an entirely new rocket must be built for each flight.

Now for the first time in history, rocket stages are starting to land with precise guidance after flight, either on a special landing platform in the ocean or by turning around and flying back to land. This allows rockets to be reused—a major step in making it easier to get to space.

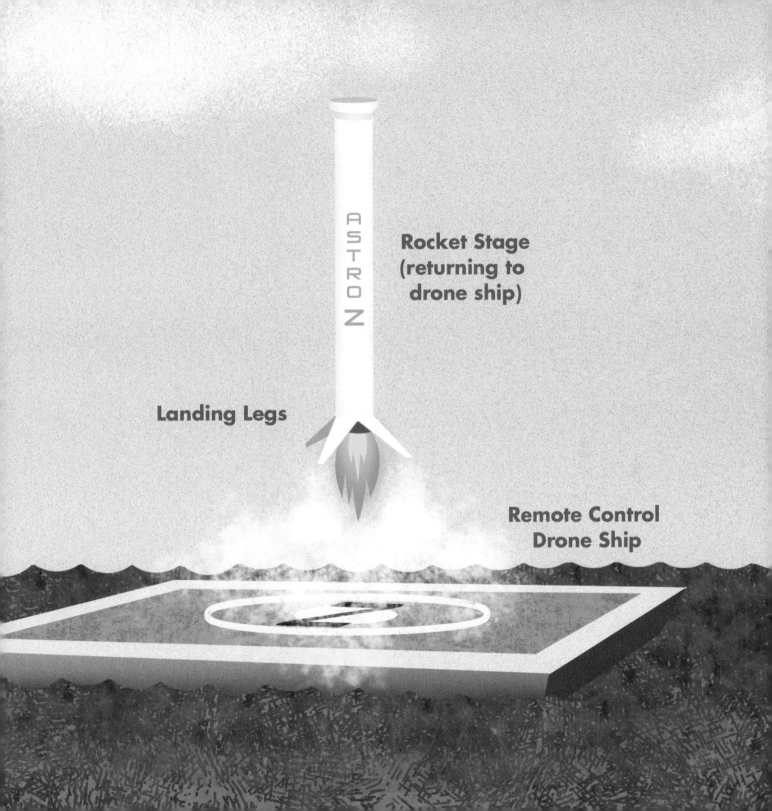

Orbits

For rockets and spacecraft,
the hardest part is not getting
to space, but staying up there.
Even in space, gravity
pulls spacecraft down
toward Earth,
just like it pulls you
and other objects
toward the ground.

But if a spacecraft is
moving very, very fast,
by the time it would
normally hit the ground,
the ground is no longer there.

Orbital Path

Suborbital Path

This type of curved path is called an "orbit". In orbit, spacecraft move ten times faster than a speeding bullet: around 5 miles per second! That's 300 times faster than a car on a highway, or 30 times faster than an airplane in the sky.

Since a spacecraft in an orbit is in constant freefall toward Earth, it feel like there's no gravity in space, even though there is.

The International Space Station

Right now there's a space station up in the sky above your head, orbiting our planet. People get there by traveling in a small spaceship launched on top of a giant rocket.

The astronauts floating around on the space station need lots of supplies like food, water, clothes, and equipment for science experiments. We send supplies to the space station using cargo ships that are steered by computers and remotely controlled from the ground. Then astronauts on the space station steer the ships into a smooth docking, sometimes with the help of a robotic arm.

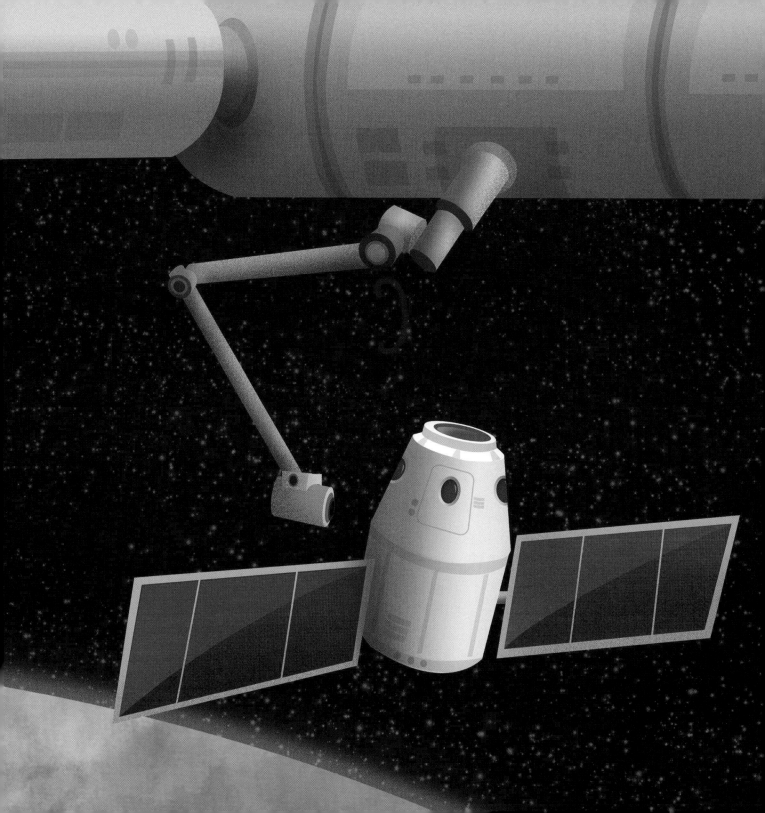

Going to the Moon

In order to send astronauts beyond Earth orbit, we need a really big rocket. In the 1960s and 1970s, NASA used the largest rocket ever built, Saturn V, to send 27 people to the Moon over 9 missions. Saturn V rockets were enormous— as tall as skyscrapers. This was called the Apollo program, and each flight used a series of spacecraft in order to reduce weight as much as possible in each segment of the mission.

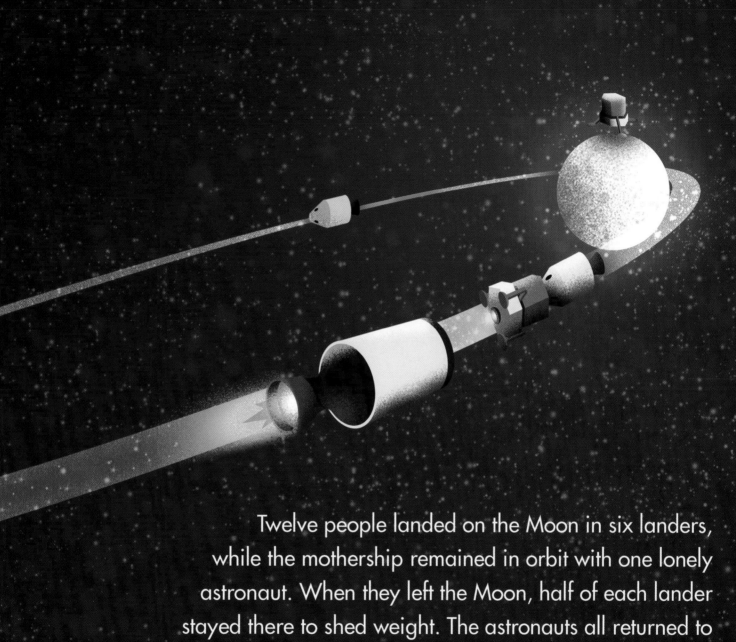

Twelve people landed on the Moon in six landers,
while the mothership remained in orbit with one lonely
astronaut. When they left the Moon, half of each lander
stayed there to shed weight. The astronauts all returned to
Earth in a tiny gumdrop-shaped spacecraft no larger than
a minivan. Everything else had been discarded along the way.

Going to Mars

Getting to planets like Mars works the same way as getting to the Moon, except that it takes a much longer time. Mars is 142 times farther than the Moon—and that's at closest approach. Since both Earth and Mars orbit the Sun, the distance and time to travel between them varies based on their positions. Earth takes 365 days (1 year) to circle the Sun, but Mars takes 687 days.

To get from Earth to Mars, first you have to get to Earth orbit. Then from there, you fire your engine to escape Earth's gravity and send you on a path to Mars. This is still an orbit, but an orbit of the Sun. Once your spacecraft reaches Mars, you need to slow down to enter Mars orbit before you can land.

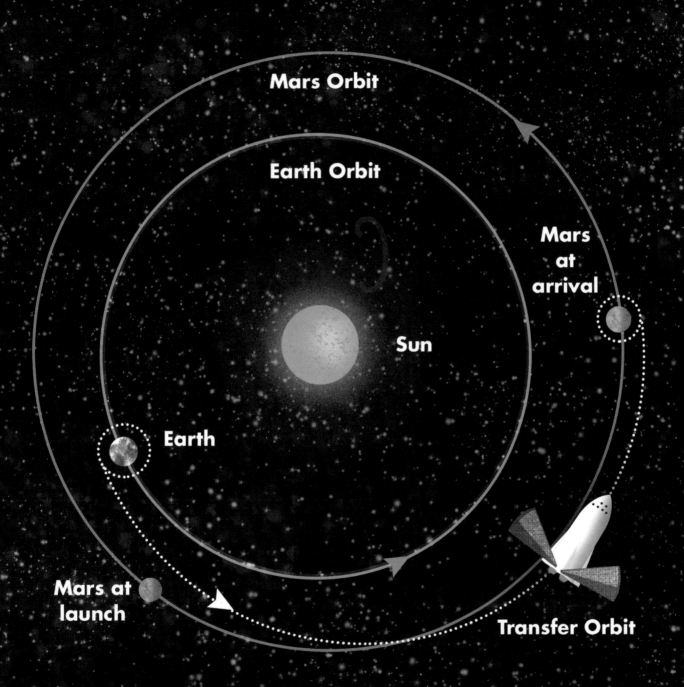

Exploring Mars

Over the years, we have sent more than 50 robotic missions to Mars, with around half of these successful (getting to Mars is hard!). In fact, there are several robots exploring Mars right now! Some of these observe the planet from orbit, others land in place, and some have wheels to drive around.

Perhaps life once existed on Mars, and maybe some microbes still do. Our robotic explorers are looking for water on Mars, and searching for signs of life now or in the past. Someday soon, humans will land on Mars. It's the closest planet we could live on, but you would still need to create oxygen to breathe from Mars' thin carbon dioxide atmosphere, and melt ice to make drinking water.

Ion Engines

Ion engines use electricity to accelerate positively charged ions toward a negatively charged grid at extremely high speeds of up to 90,000 miles per hour. That's more than 50 times faster than a speeding bullet! Since they use only tiny particles as fuel, ion engines are very efficient for deep space travel.

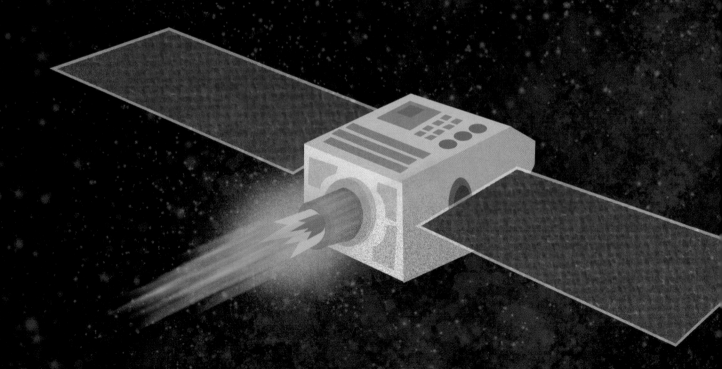

This type of engine was used by NASA's Dawn spacecraft to visit the asteroid Vesta and dwarf planet Ceres. The largest of the asteroids, Ceres is a giant ice cube about a third the size of the Moon, or a tenth the size of Earth.

Soon we might be able to mine asteroids for water, rocket fuel, and minerals that could be valuable for building distant outposts across the solar system. If you lived on an asteroid base, you wouldn't need a rocket to fly in space—you could just jump!

Solar Sails

The light and heat of the Sun is carried by tiny
invisible particles called "photons", and each of these applies
a tiny push. Individually, this push is too small to be felt,
but if you collect enough photons, you can propel a spacecraft.
A solar sail is a very large but very light surface used to
capture as many photons as possible.

Solar sails might have to be miles across to capture enough
photons to propel a large spacecraft, but since there is nothing in
space to slow you down, you could reach very high speeds. Best of
all, they use no fuel, so they never stop working. This means that
they could someday be used to propel a spacecraft to another star, a
voyage that could take hundreds of years.

Gravity Slingshots

To get to planets far out from the Sun, we have to move really fast—even faster than a rocket. Spacecraft build up speed by flying past a planet really close, using the planet's gravity to "slingshot" deep out into space. The planet is very heavy, so gravity tugs the spacecraft, flinging it on its way.

Earth

Jupiter

Pull of gravity

Extra speed

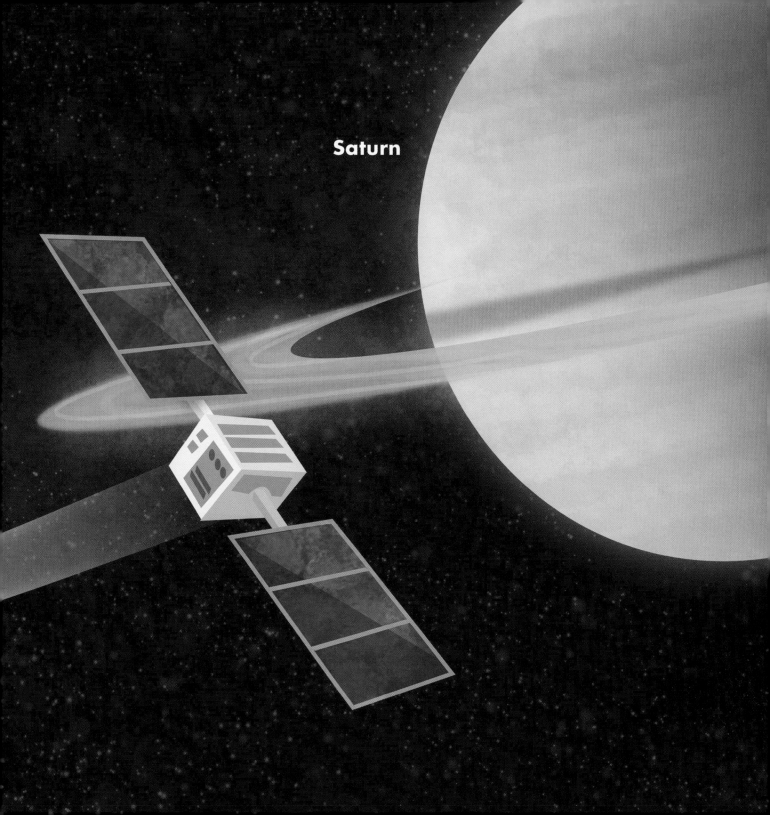

Jupiter

Jupiter is the largest planet, almost like a miniature star. In fact, it's so large and so far from the Sun that it creates more heat than it receives. A giant ball of swirling gas, Jupiter could fit 1,300 Earths inside. It features a "Giant Red Spot", a storm the size of Earth that has lasted for more than 300 years!

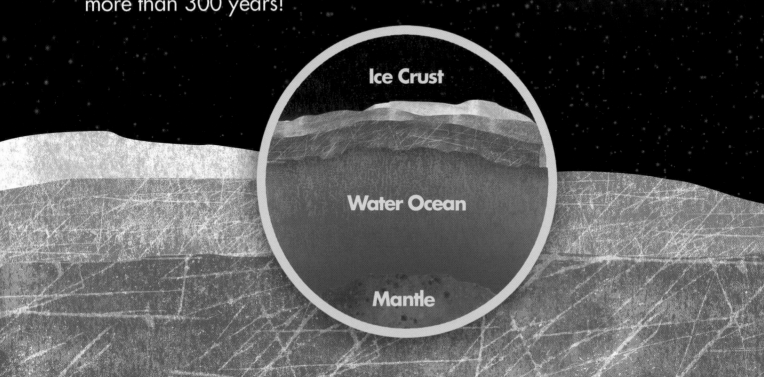

Ice Crust

Water Ocean

Mantle

Jupiter has a mini "solar system" of its own, with at least 67 moons. Some of these are really interesting, like Io, the most volcanic world in the solar system, and Europa, the largest skating rink, with a sheet of ice covering the entire moon. It seems Europa supports an ocean under the ice, with more water than all the oceans of Earth. It may even have life swimming below in the depths.

Several spacecraft have visited the Jupiter system, including the two Voyagers (1979), Galileo (1995-2003), and Juno (2016-2021). More missions are planned to the gas giant and its moons, including a lander on Europa that will look for signs of life rising up through the ice from the ocean below.

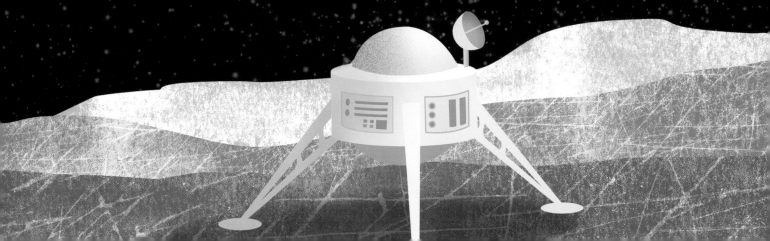

Saturn

Saturn is the second largest planet in the solar system, known for its giant rings. Like Jupiter, Saturn also has a mini "solar system" of its own, supporting over 50 moons. Two of these are especially interesting, and were explored in detail by the Cassini spacecraft, which orbited Saturn between 2004 and 2017.

Titan

Enceladus is a small icy moon that supports a subsurface liquid ocean, geysers of water and ice particles trailing into space, and possibly life. Saturn's largest moon Titan is larger than Earth's Moon, and is one of the most Earthlike worlds in the solar system. It's the only other place with lakes of liquid on its surface, but Titan's lakes are filled with liquid methane at extremely cold temperatures (–290 °F/–179 °C). Titan also has an atmosphere very similar to Earth's in thickness and composition

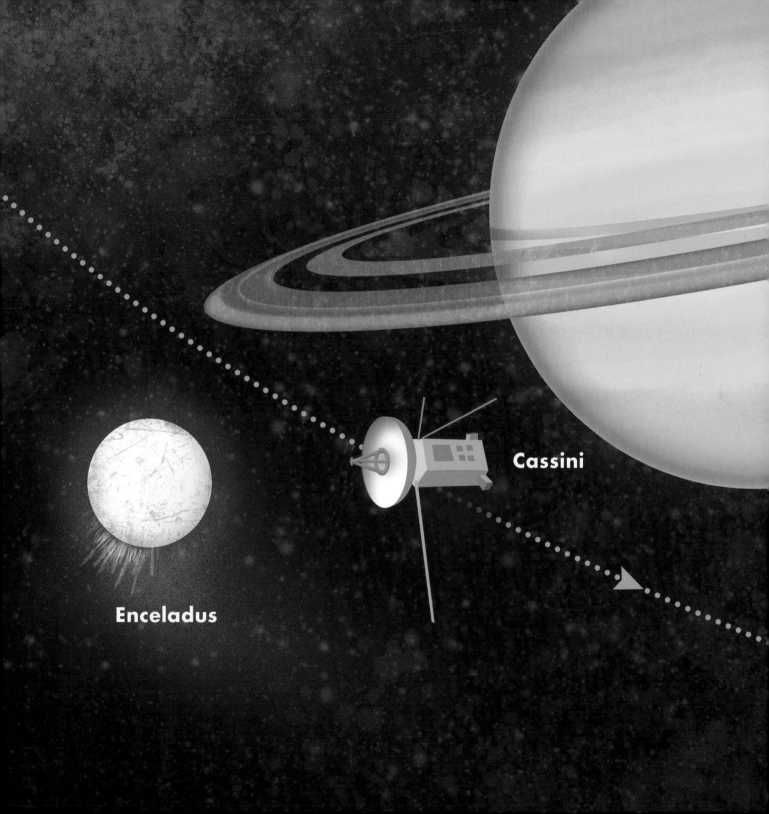

Ice Giants

Uranus and Neptune are a bit like Jupiter and Saturn,
but because they contain more water, ammonia, and methane
ice, they're sometimes called "Ice Giants". Each has several
moons of its own, the most interesting being Neptune's Triton,
which orbits in the opposite direction of most worlds
in the solar system.

In the 1970s and 1980s, there was a relative alignment of the planets, which made it possible to visit all at the same time. Two Voyager spacecraft were launched, and Voyager 2 took the first close-up images of the Ice Giants and their moons. The Voyagers are now the farthest-ever objects built by humans, traveling into the depths of interstellar space.

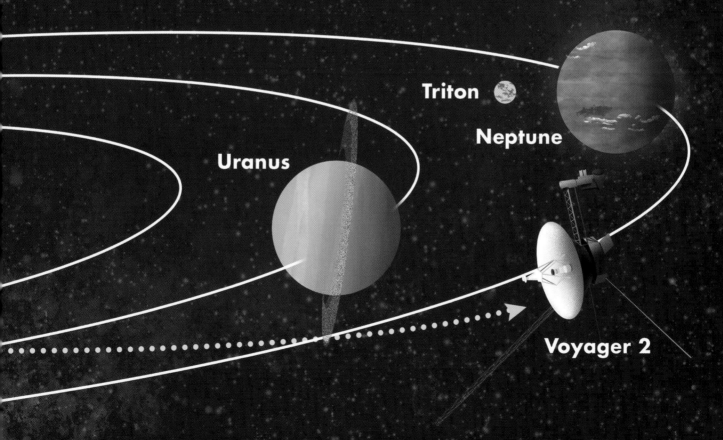

Uranus

Triton

Neptune

Voyager 2

The Kuiper Belt

Beyond Neptune lies the Kuiper Belt, a region of mysterious
icy worlds so far away that the Sun provides less light than
a full Moon on Earth. Pluto was the first Kuiper Belt object
to be discovered, in 1930. Pluto is a bit smaller than Earth's
Moon, but has five moons of its own, including Charon,
which is half the size of Pluto itself. In 2015, the
New Horizons spacecraft became first to visit Pluto,
giving us a close-up look at its shape, composition,
and internal structure.

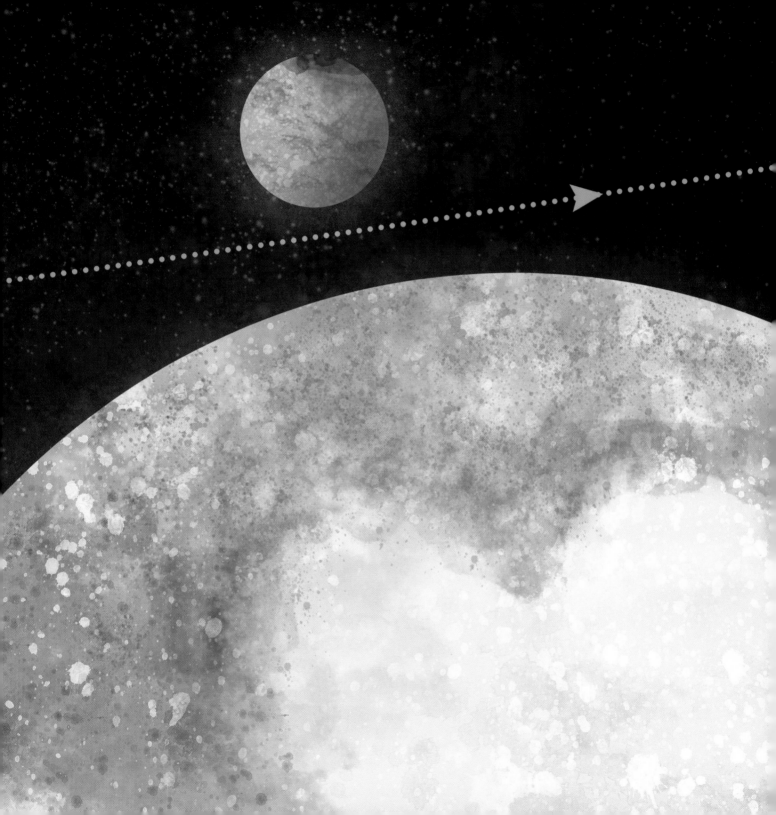

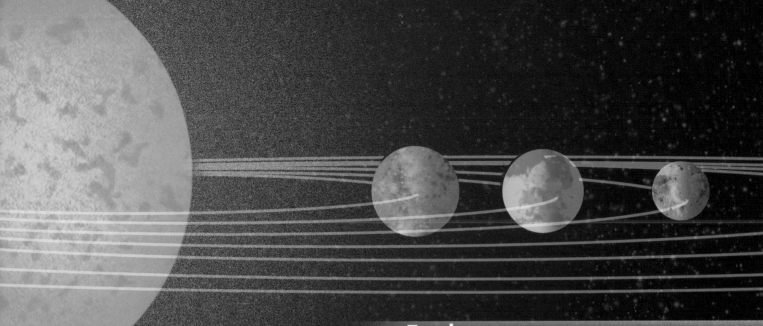

Too hot

Exoplanets

Our solar system is just one of hundreds of billions in our galaxy, and our galaxy is one among hundreds of billions in the Universe. We think that most stars are circled by planets, and since these don't orbit our Sun, we call them "exoplanets". The main way we find exoplanets is by staring at the star they orbit and looking for a slight wobble caused by the planet's gravity, or by looking for a slight dimming of the star as the planet passes in front. This is a bit like looking for a fly passing in front of a searchlight on the other side of the world.

Just right (habitable zone)   **Too cold**

Many exoplanets are boiling hot or freezing cold, but at least some are the right distance from their star to have oceans of liquid water on their surface, like Earth. We think that worlds with liquid water should be habitable—meaning that they could support life. Some solar systems would be very different than ours. A dim star might have habitable planets closer than Mercury is to our Sun. Some stars might have several habitable planets, like TRAPPIST-1, which has seven planets that we know of, three of which are in the habitable zone.

Extraterrestrial Life

Are we alone in the Universe? We don't know for sure. We think that life should be able to exist on many other planets out there, and simple life forms should even be able to live on places in our solar system like Mars, Europa, or Enceladus. If we found life on one of these worlds, it would suggest that life often arises when the conditions are right. This would mean that life is common throughout the Universe.

What about intelligent life, like the aliens of science fiction? It is certainly possible that there are other intelligent beings out there that we may someday meet. Even on our own planet there are animals that are fairly intelligent, like chimpanzees, elephants, dolphins, and octopuses.

With modern technology, radio signals from Earth have now been traveling out into space for over a century. Someday, these might be picked up by someone. In the meantime, we scan the skies for signals from other beings like us, somewhere out there across the vastness of space.

OUR OTHER BOOKS:

ANDREW RADER IS AN AEROSPACE ENGINEER, AUTHOR, AND GAME DESIGNER FROM CANADA BUT BASED AT SPACEX IN LOS ANGELES. HE'S AN AVID TRIVIA PLAYER, SPACE AND MARS ENTHUSIAST, SCIENCE NERD, HISTORY BUFF, AND INCURABLE KNOW-IT-ALL.

GALEN FRAZER IS A GRAPHIC ARTIST AND SELF-PROCLAIMED SPACE GEEK BASED IN THE BALTIMORE AREA. WHEN NOT ILLUSTRATING TOTALLY RAD SPACE BOOKS, HE ENJOYS SPENDING TIME WITH HIS FAMILY AND PLAYING GUITAR.